TURNING PASSION INTO PROFESSION:

How to Make Money through Blogs

SIMPLE BUSINESS

CHAPTER 1

IS IT POSSIBLE TO MAKE MONEY WITH A BLOG?

People say money makes the world go around. While there's some truth to it, there are still some people who don't want to admit how much they need it to survive and live to the fullest.

Everybody wants to make money. It's precise because every single thing has a currency nowadays. We're not living in the olden days anymore, wherein people can just trade their goods for something. Now, the economy is anchored on banks, loans, investments, and cash. The value of a nation's currency is measured based on its local and global performance.

The reality now is that, as the whole world advances, competition in the market also increases. The price for everything becomes more expensive, and that's why it's normal for people nowadays to overwork, find a second or third job, or create a small business. We do this just so we can earn additional income. After all, who knows how expensive everything will be in a few decades?

Thanks to the gift of technology, a lot of people all over the world can already earn money online. YouTubers, online businesses, and freelancers are some examples of those who do. Thanks to the internet, people are now finding more ways to earn income from the web, ways that people think is supposed to be impossible.

One of those ways is through **blogging**. "What?" You might say. "Can I really earn money just by *blogging*?" Yes, you definitely can! You just need to be educated with how to's, tips, and different methods.

You might be wondering, "How do I get started? Where will I learn everything that I need to know?" Don't worry! Today is your lucky day. This short e-book will discuss all the fundamentals of making money through blogs. You don't have to worry about sifting through different references; everything you need to know can be found in the next few pages. In a short nick of time, you'll be able to earn some cash just by typing on your laptop or computer. The greatest thing about it is that you can do this while you're in the comforts of your own home, with a flexible schedule that only *you* can control.

THE WORLD'S MOST PROFITABLE BLOGS IN THE INTERNET

Before we can get started with the basics, it's important to get an idea of how successful you can be when you start pursuing blogging as one of your money-makers. Don't worry, we won't get much into the details. We just need to briefly see how blog sites excelled in getting more profit and attention. With that, here are some of the world's most successful and profitable blogs:

1. Huffington Post (recently renamed as HuffPost)

Started up by Ariana Huffington on May 2005, with an estimated monthly revenue of 14 million dollars, HuffPost is an online blog site that revolves around the niche of politics. Sometimes, it serves as an alternative to other news sources, and even expanding to several topics that are not political. This blog site pays content makers and individual bloggers to garner more diverse content. Because of this, they're able to publish many articles consistently on a daily basis. If you feel like your content is in line with HuffPost, then perhaps you can consider starting out here to get some reputable experience.

2. Mashable

Founded by Pete Cashmore in 2005 when he was just 19 years old (it seems 2005 may have been a great year for starting up blog sites), Mashable evolved from a simple blog site for social media enthusiasts and tech-savvies, to a global media company that aims to transform human interactions and reshape culture in this modern-day of technology. Since then, Mashable has gained more attention by partnering up with social networking sites like Twitter and Facebook where it gets a huge amount of its traffic from.

How do you feel upon knowing that Pete Cashmore made this when he was just 19? Surely, this is a prime example of somebody who was able to transform his passion into his source of income, all the while providing top-notch tech content to people around the world. Who wouldn't be inspired by this?

3. **PerezHilton.com**

Made by Mario Lavandeira (yes, Perez Hilton's real name), this controversial blog site is known for notoriously covering celebrity news and gossip. Still, the site was originally meant to be Perez's online journal and "diary". However, in an interview with *Cliché Magazine* in 2010, he stated that the reason why he shifted from discussing personal topics to showbiz was that celebrities were "far more entertaining" then his life.

Yes, there is a never-ending debate whether this blog site has broken barriers of privacy for celebrities and other media personalities, but many people are still invested in knowing about their lives. Still, one cannot deny the success and attention that this site garnered, despite its infamous reputation of barging into celebrities' lives.

4. **TechCrunch**

Known for its great reputation for publishing honest, objective reviews of tech products, this site was originally formed by journalists Keith Teare and Michael Arrington in 2005 (yes, 2005 again!). In 2010, it was then bought by AOL, formerly known as America

Online. More than boasting their well-respected profiles of tech products and businesses, it also reports about the business aspects of technology, trends, as well as current tech news. With this, don't be surprised that they'll be the first ones to give updates about to-be-released Apple products!

Just like Mashable, it has found its niche and gathered a loyal group of tech-savvy readers, or just about anyone who's looking for reputable product reviews. TechCrunch is a great example of finding a blog site's niche and succeeding from there. Finding a great niche will be further discussed in the third chapter.

5. Smashing Magazine

In 2006, Vitaly Friedman and Sven Lennartz created this blog site specifically for web designers and developers. The site prides itself on delivering quality content, focusing on "delivering reliable, useful, and practical articles" for this interested in it. Unlike the HuffPost, Smashing Magazine does not have a big team. Instead, they concentrate on building a small, tight-knitted the community of passionate content creators. More than just producing blogs, they also produce digital books, as well as hold job openings, conferences, and membership.

The activity of the Smashing Magazine team is a great example of expanding their blog site's horizons by creating different products and seeking different ways of earning profit. These different ways will be further tackled in the fourth chapter.

IS IT GOOD FOR ME?

Of course, it is! What's greater than being able to work everywhere, instead of being cramped in a small cubicle in a cold office department? What's greater than having the freedom to pursue your passion and control your own time? What's greater than eventually becoming your *own boss*?

Yes, it may seem too good to be true. Still, whether you're a housewife (or househusband—let's not forget them), a part-time office worker, a businessperson, or a hobbyist, blogging is perfect for anyone who can write about the things they're passionate about. As long as you have a laptop or computer, some guts, and a great amount of dedication, you're good to go!

If you're a housewife, for example, you can write your own blogs while the kids are away in school, and you'll even get an extra income. If you're a person with an online business, you can promote it in your blog site and get new customers from it. If you're a hobbyist or a craftsperson, you can share your knowledge and help other people learn the craft. This is why blogging is such a great way to get more attention to the things you're passionate about, not to mention the numerous advantages it can give you on top of making more cash.

Besides the flexible time schedule and the extra profit, you can hone your writing skills and enhance your knowledge, too. That experience is crucial, especially for somebody who's looking forward to working for bigger companies or expanding their business. More than that, it's easy to manage once you got the hang of it, especially when you create your blog site with user-friendly templates just like in WordPress or Wix (more on that later). Another advantage would be the fact that you get to establish more connections with other people—people who share the same passion as you, and people who can also help you accelerate your career or business, whatever that may be.

Of course, it will not be an easy journey: nevertheless, just by simply allotting a couple hours of your weekly free time into writing blogs, you get to earn extra cash on top of your primary job.

If you're in university or high school, you can allot the profit you earned from blogging into your allowance, dorm fees, or hobbies. It's really no different than your typical school project. While we're all living in a world where prices and market competition are ever-increasing, blogging is one of the smartest ways you can do to prepare yourself for the future, while having to rely less and less on bank loans or debts.

Now that you've been introduced to the many possibilities of making money through blogging, let's get to the step-by-step procedure of starting up your own blog.

CHAPTER 2

HOW TO START A BLOG

For this chapter, we will go into detail how you can start a blog.

Here, you have two options—to create your site in (1) free platforms, or (2) self-hosted platforms.

Before we could dive into that, you have to know a couple of things.

First, you need to think about your niche. Your "niche" is a general topic that your blog would revolve around, whether it be health, technology, fashion, celebrity, craft making, etc. Think about what you're truly passionate about.

You have to keep that in mind when you start to design your blog site and think about your style of writing, with full knowledge of who your readers will be. Of course, we will thoroughly discuss this step in Chapter 3, but essentially, you need to ask yourself this question: *what would my blog be about?*

Second, think about your host. Of course, you may opt to design a website from scratch, and that is only if you're knowledgeable about programming, codes, and computer languages like HTML and JavaScript. Definitely, not everyone has the time to make a website all on their own, and that's why you can choose from the many platforms online, complete with user-friendly templates and basic codes.

WEB HOSTING

From here, you might start to feel a little overwhelmed with the "techy" terms; however, in order to start your own blog site, you need to understand how web hosting works. Moreover, you also need to know the most popular and reliable web hosts there is, like BlueHost.

When you start your own website, you will start uploading a lot of things there, like your blog articles. Every content on your site is considered as "data", something which needs to be stored somewhere. This is why you need a **web host.** The host's main job is to store all of your website data on a server, and keep it available for access by people around the world, through several browsers like Google, Safari, and Mozilla Firefox.

The thing is, the average person doesn't have any server. Chances are, *you* also don't have a server, especially if you're just blogging at home. Most businesses also don't even have their own servers, which is why they also need to purchase web hosting services from companies that provide that.

Web hosting is the most essential concept for blogging. It's basically the "powerhouse" of any website. You will need a server to store all your website data, just like how you'll need to rent an apartment where you can live and put your things.

If you're wondering what a server looks like, it's basically a physical computer which oddly looks like a large CPU. You might have watched action or spy movies like *Mission: Impossible*, where the secret agent infiltrates a "server room" to gain access to the enemy's data-filled with, say, nuclear codes. So, when you purchase a web hosting service, you're essentially buying space in that server room, where you can put all your data for as long as your website is accessible.

WHAT MAKES A GOOD WEB HOST?

When starting out your blog site, it may be wise to do a quick research of possible hosting providers. Although some sites like WordPress have already partnered up with reputable web hosts (so you don't really have to choose), you might want to know the criteria for choosing a good web host when you want to switch to an independent domain. Perhaps, you may even want to create your own independent website right from the start.

The first criterium is called the **uptime.** "Uptime" is essentially something that measures how reliable the device or system is. Also known as the opposite of "downtime", you may want to pick a web host with reputable uptime. After all, what's the use of your blog site if users can't access it most of the time? Uptime is usually measured in percentages, and take note: 99% uptime (1% downtime) still means that your site will be down at an average of 72 hours per month. Likewise, 99.9% uptime (0.1% downtime) corresponds to 43 minutes of downtime per month.

Every person will have a different preference for how much downtime is acceptable for them, but it's also definitely related to what kind your website is, and how much traffic it receives every time. Don't worry, if you're just starting out your blog site, 99% uptime is still highly acceptable. That said, 99% of uptime should always be your minimum.

Usually, web hosting service providers calculate their uptime, but it's not always accurate. You can measure it yourself just to make sure. From time to time, check your website and see if it's up and running. Furthermore, there are also third-party uptime monitoring services that can be found online, such as *pingdom.com*, *serviceuptime.com*, *uptimerobot.com*, and *internetseer.com*. You just simply have to provide your domain, and the sites will work its magic for you.

Second, you also have to look at the **loading speed** of the web host. This is the second most important criteria. Your blog site may be up and running, but maybe it's too slow to load. Perhaps, for once in your life, you find yourself annoyed at how slow a specific website loads, to the point that you just exited the tab before getting the chance to properly view it. Uptime and load speed work hand-in-hand when it comes to guaranteeing you more traffic and more visitors.

After conducting research, Google states that the acceptable average loading speed for a website is 2 seconds or 2000 ms. If it takes longer than 3 seconds, visitors will most likely give up and exit your site. Of course, not everyone will leave after those 3 precious seconds, but you will certainly receive fewer visitors. According to a scientific study by Geoff Kenyon, if your site loads after barely 3 seconds (or 2.9 seconds, specifically), your website is faster than 50% of the total web pages in the world. Keep this in mind. Choose a web host with a fast loading speed if you want to have happy users. Like uptime monitoring services, you can also search online sites that can measure loading speed for you. *WhichLoadsFaster.com* is one of your many options.

The third criteria is the web host's **introductory pricing**. Of course, getting a web host for your site will cost you some money. Usually, it charges you for a monthly subscription. There are definitely "free web hosting plans" available for you, like in WordPress; but of course, there are some limitations to it especially when it comes to earning profit through website ads.

Fourth, you also need to look at its **security options**. Web hosting service providers usually have good security features available for you and for your site. This is highly crucial, especially when protecting you and your users' personal information from hackers who might want to get into your site, scam you, and even victimize you and others with phishing. More specifically, you might want to look into whether the web host provides you an SSL certificate. An SSL certificate is something that enables your blog site to be more secured, particularly to evolve from "HTTP" to "HTTPS", which includes data encryptions. If your site does not begin with "https", then there's a higher risk for interception or eavesdropping by hackers and other unwanted people.

Fifth, you'd want to check if they have a **flexible variety of plans**. Since you're just starting out with your blog site, you'll be at that period of exploring the many possibilities for your site, as well as build a good reputation while gathering a stable number of visitors. As your blog site grows in content, size, and popularity, you might want to consider upgrading to better hosting plans. When you're already at that phase, you'll need a smooth and quick transition from one plan to another.

Next, you also need to check if there is a **30-day money-back guarantee** for your web host. In other words, it's like a "warranty" for their hosting service. Within those 30 days, you are allowed to check whether the web host performance is up to or above par. When the 30 days are up, you can decide whether you're satisfied with their service. If not, you can get a refund (although usually not 100%) and then find another web host that's better suited for you.

The sixth criteria is **ample resources** for beginners. You'll want a web host account that's intuitive, easy to understand, and essentially, "beginner-friendly". You might need to check if they have a "how to get started" manual somewhere in their interface, or some kind of initial tutorial guide, just like whenever you download a brand-new software. Does it have a "Help Center" button somewhere?

Supported website migration is also something that you need to look into. Of course, when you begin creating your website, all data will be stored up in the web host's server. When you decide to "migrate" from one web hosting platform to another, especially because you're dissatisfied with your current web host, there will be a whole intricate process that needs to take place. Most importantly, your ocean of data will have to be transferred to your new host's server.

Check into the "migration" process of the web hosts. You'll want a simple, quick, and pain-free process, so you'll be able to concentrate on your blog faster. There are web hosts that won't charge you with a "migration fee", but there are also some that do. They will, after all, lose a client.

Last, you also have to consider its **customer support**. Does it offer email ticket support, live chat, or even phone support? Is it 24/7 customer service? The last thing you'll want is to be awake up at night and find that your website is down, then have your frustration be aggravated when you find out that customer service is also *down*. Of course, you want these web pages errors fixed quickly and painlessly, else you might lose some visitors.

There you go. The nine criteria for what makes a good web host were briefly explained for your convenience. As you start researching for possible web hosts, always keep these in your mind. You'd want something that can give you smooth, carefree website management in the long run; something that doesn't take up too much time, that you're bothered whenever you're adding or editing content in your site. Furthermore, constantly remember that choosing your web hosting service provider is more than just thinking about how much it's good for starting up websites. You also have to think about the future, and whether that web host can meet your needs when the future comes.

DIFFERENT KINDS OF WEB HOSTING

In the previous section, it was mentioned that it's crucial to know whether a certain web host can offer you a variety of plans. Now, let's get into detail about what those "plans" are.

Essentially, these "plans" can also be referred to as the different kinds of web hosting. As of now, there are four (4) kinds, namely: shared hosting, VPS hosting, dedicated hosting, and cloud hosting.

First, what is **shared hosting**? This is usually what beginner website owners use, simply because they're in that period of "trying things out". Basically, shared hosting is when many websites—it can be 100, 1000, or even 5000 websites—share only ONE server. Definitely, there are pros and cons to this one. For its advantages, shared hosting is the most economical or "cheap" option out of all kinds, for the mere fact that you won't really take up one whole server just for your website. It is also the safest option for websites that are still in development. Of course, you wouldn't want to pay for a bigger server slot when your website has not gained enough traction yet, right? On the other hand, shared hosting might not be the most ideal especially when you've gained more visitors and added more content to your websites. Given that there are hundreds or thousands of websites connected to one server, you might have to sacrifice a faster loading speed. That won't work out well for you especially when your site becomes busier.

The second type is called **VPS hosting**, short for "virtual private server" hosting. Once your site has gained some reputation, you might want to switch over to this type. VPS hosting is still a shared environment, just like the previous kind, but this time, it's now limited to a maximum of 20 websites for each server. Obviously, you'll get to enjoy faster speed and bigger server memory, on top of other added features. Not only that, but each of those 20 sites will also receive the same amount of space and memory. Now, you won't have to worry about other sites hogging most of the server space and loading speed. Some people would consider this as one of the most flexible types of web hosting.

Third, we have **dedicated hosting**. This is pretty self-explanatory, isn't it? This type allows one website for only one server. Sounds like a dream come true, yeah? It probably is, because chances are, it would mean that switching to this hosting plan signifies the ongoing success of your blog site. With that said, this is the preferred and more suitable option for sites that receive at least 100,000 visitors each month. Although, you might be a bit disadvantaged because it requires the user (you) to have some skill in computers and web hosting. It gets a little more complicated. More than that, this is obviously the more expensive plan out of all types. Still, if your website has huge hardware needs, thousands of visitors, and large data, or if your site prioritizes data safety and confidentiality, you might want to opt for this one.

Last, we have **cloud hosting**. Arguably, cloud hosting is deemed as the most reliable and flexible option. Basically, it's an "upgraded version" of the VPS hosting, but this time, the physical servers are divided into different cloud clusters. In this way, your website can be hosted on multiple servers. So, when one "cluster" is down, perhaps because of too much traffic, the other clusters can shoulder that extra work. Your site will still work just fine. This is the best option for large, multinational companies because it provides a variety of options for computer security. Most importantly, the system of cloud hosting is designed to withstand, and even prevent attacks from hackers. Why? It's because when one server is hacked, the website owner can reconfigure the site and still gain control of it in the end.

Choosing your web hosting plan can be initially overwhelming and complicated. However, once you know what kind of websites and circumstances a specific type of web hosting is for, you'll be able to make an easier decision on which to pick. More than that, you can even easily know when to switch plans whenever it's time for your site to be upgraded.

BLUEHOST: ONE OF THE BEST WEB HOSTING SERVICE PROVIDERS

There are lots of web hosts to choose from, but one of the most popular ones is called **BlueHost**.

First of all, let's briefly look into its background. In 2003, BlueHost was founded by Matt Heaton and Danny Ashworth in Provo, Utah. As of now, this web host powers over two million websites all over the world, empowering online users with the necessary tools to create and maintain their websites. More than that, BlueHost has partnered with WordPress and has been maintaining that relationship for over ten years now. There are many other famous websites that BlueHost powers, which makes it arguably the best web hosting service provider on the internet as of the moment.

Let's try to review BlueHost by applying some of the criteria we've discussed in the previous section.

1. **99.99% Uptime throughout the year.** BlueHost boasts 99.99% uptime all-year round. This means that there are only 8 seconds of downtime daily, which translates to 56 seconds weekly, 4 minutes monthly, and approximately 48 minutes yearly. The data is pretty great. If you choose BlueHost as your web hosting service provider, this means that your site won't even be down for more than an hour annually.

2. **The average loading speed of 0.5 seconds.** After checking with *pingdom*.com, the data shows that from July 2019 to June 2020, BlueHost as an average loading speed of 500ms or 0.5 seconds. Within that time period, the month with the fastest average loading speed was in August 2019, with 351ms or 0.35 seconds. Without a doubt, BlueHost is definitely "up there" when it comes to loading speed.

3. **Offers three out of four hosting types.** Although BlueHost doesn't offer cloud hosting, it still offers shared hosting ($2.75/month), VPS hosting ($18.99), and dedicated hosting ($79.99). The price might be shocking, yes, but as a start, you can always opt with shared hosting.

4. **Provides SSL certificate for all plans.** BlueHost already has reputable security features, and to be given an SSL certificate no matter what plan you avail is an added bonus. This ensures that your site will not be easily infiltrated by people who want to scam, hack, or phish.

5. **Offers 30-day money-back guarantee.** This is pretty self-explanatory, don't you think?

6. **User-friendly interface.** Unlike other web hosts, BlueHost is relatively easy to use especially for those who are just starting up their websites. Just a few clicks here and there make for uncomplicated website management.

7. **24/7 customer service!** Rest assured, whenever you're faced with hosting problems, you can easily contact their team for help. Not only that, but they also provide customer support in different kinds: live chat, email, and even support.

Of course, a couple of disadvantages, too. For one, BlueHost will charge you a whopping $149.99 when you decide to migrate your site. Second, it also charges a high renewal rate, although this is a common phenomenon among other web hosting service providers. Still, because BlueHost is a highly reputable web host, and that the pros outweigh the cons, the internet community still widely deems it as one of the best. Of course, WordPress has a couple of other web host partners (not to mention that you can basically choose any web host for your WordPress site), but BlueHost is still one of the most reliable out there. Plus, it offers FREE domain name and email, among a few other things.

WHERE TO START MY BLOG?

As mentioned before, unless you're someone who's adept in a programming language, you might want to find a site that offers beginner-friendly website builder. One of the best sites on the internet is called **WordPress**.

You've probably heard this a lot of times from other people or visited a site with "wordpress.com" at the end of the URL. It was founded by Matt Mullenweg and Mike Little in 2003 and has now grown to become one of the leading website builders on the internet. As of now, it powers 37% of the whole web, so it has had a great reputation for many years now.

How do you start your blog here? First of all, you have to **pick which web host you want** for your site. We've briefly discussed BlueHost, but know that there's also another option. Still, as a beginner, know that you can never go wrong with BlueHost!

Second, you have to **purchase your hosting plan**. We've thoroughly elaborated on the different kinds of web hosting, so right now, you should know what would be best for you. As mentioned before, the safest bet for you is to avail shared hosting plan. It's the least expensive option, too.

The next thing you have to do is to **create and purchase your domain**. Some web hosts would charge you an extra fee for that (an average of $10), but if you chose BlueHost, you can get your domain for free. Now, just in case you don't know what a domain is, it's like your website's "permanent address", to put it simply. This is the link that people type or click on when trying to access your blog.

An example of a domain name could be "johnapplesmith.wordpress.com", just like what you'd see at the top of every web browser. As much as possible, your domain name should match the name of your blog; therefore, it might be best to start thinking of an appropriate name for your site beforehand, assuming you've already found your niche.

When picking your domain name, you have to make sure that it's available across all social media platforms, too. This step might not be as important if you simply want to focus on promoting your blog site on your personal social media accounts. However, if you're a burgeoning business (online or physical), make sure that you can also use that domain name when you start expanding your online presence into different social networking sites.

One thing that might help you is to go to something that we call "domain name generators". There are many of these online, yet perhaps, one of the most inclusive ones is Panabee (or www.panabee.com). You just need to type in two keywords for your blog site, then it would generate available names for you. The greatest thing about Panabee is that it searches across social media and other online user community platforms, too. Because of this, you're guaranteed that the domain name will be available for your use in social media, like on Twitter, Instagram, or Facebook.

Now, when you pick your hosting plan, you'll need to enter your domain name and several pieces of information for your web hosting account. After that, you might have to **install the WordPress software**. Usually, after setting your account with the web host, it would guide through how to install WordPress.

DESIGNING MY WORDPRESS BLOG

We'll keep this part short and simple. When designing your site, you'll have access to WordPress's wide collection of plugins and themes. Themes essentially provide the "overall look" and color palette for your blog. On the other hand, plugins are things that can add functionality to your blogs (i.e. social network buttons, related tags for improved search engine optimization or SEO, et cetera).

Designing your blog site may be initially overwhelming, but it's not complicated. You'll get to see the menu bar on the left side of your screen, with buttons such as "appearance settings", "colors", "menus", and "sections" ready for your use. The interface is pretty straightforward, you just have to take the time to discover them all. Just be a little patient and enjoy the process of designing your site! It doesn't have to be stressful. Make sure the colors and fonts resonate with what your blog will be about. Remember, it's crucial to make a good first impression for your visitors. Go have fun with it!

CHAPTER 3

BEST ADVICE TO HELP YOU WITH YOUR BLOG

Congratulations! You've successfully created your blog site. Now, it's time for you to start adding some content to it. For this chapter, you will only be given three tips — the best ones - to ensure success for your blog. Those are consistency, motivation, and a great niche.

CONSISTENCY

Your blogsite will require maintenance. From here on out, challenges are only just starting. You'll need to consistently produce blog posts, else your visitors won't have anything to read. It's akin to having a YouTube channel, yet not posting any videos on it. Of course, you won't get any traffic or "views", if there's nothing to watch. Likewise, your blog site won't get popular if there are no blog posts.

Determine how often you want to post. Of course, you'll need to add this to your weekly schedule, so make sure that the frequency is feasible and easy to commit on. As a start, it would be nice to post every 3 to 5 days, but once a week is also a great frequency. Incorporate some time into your weekly routine for writing blog posts.

Plan out your content. Before starting your blog site, it's smart to list out categories of things you can talk about. For example, if your blog is about movie reviews, you might want to make subcategories like these: individual movie reviews, all-time favorites, top ten movies for a specific genre, movie of the month, to-be-watched list, etc. That way, you'll never run out of content.

You might notice that it's really similar to maintaining a YouTube channel. For example, a typical YouTube channel focusing on health and wellness would have workout videos, tips, common misconceptions about exercises, HIIT (or high-intensity interval training), healthy meals, meal plans, etc. Likewise, your blog should have something like this.

At the end of the day, remember that if you're not consistent with blog posting, you also won't get consistent visitors. It will be harder for you to build dedicated or avid readers of your blog, especially when trying to earn money based on how many people viewed ads on your site.

MOTIVATION

At some point in your blogging career, things will start feeling like a "task", or like some tedious work. This would be bad for you and your blog, especially since it would undoubtedly affect the quality of your content. You'll feel like you're stuck in a rut.

When you're starting to feel like this, **always remember why you're passionate about it.** Whether you created your blog for your online business, for your hobbies, etc, it's always good to have a goal in mind. Definitely, you won't easily earn money within just one night. You first need to build a reputation and constantly work for that goal. Make no mistake, even though blogging is not an easy way for you to earn money in the beginning, everything will be worth it once you've gained some traction. Don't be easily discouraged when you feel like you're not seeing results. It just means that the results aren't there *yet*. Wait for a little more until you experience that.

Balance out your life. Just like anything else, you shouldn't make blogging your life. It shouldn't consume all of your energy and time. It should just be a small part of your life, lest you'll feel burnt out and unmotivated. While you're blogging, make sure that you're still experiencing the best way your know-how. Get some inspiration. Take some time out for yourself. Spend quality time with your family and friends! Watch some Netflix for the heck of it. The more great things you experience in your life outside of blogging, the more you'll feel motivated to work on your blog.

Keep doing things that would add to your content. This may seem self-explanatory, but how can you write blog posts when you don't have anything to write about? Let's go back to that one example wherein your blog is all about movie reviews. How can you review a film when you haven't watched one recently? How can you produce your "movie of the month" blog post when you don't make enough time for you to sit down and watch? It's just as simple as that. Blogging is more than just *producing* content; it's also about constantly discovering and learning things that could all be a potential blog post. You will inevitably feel unmotivated when you don't have anything to talk about. In the end, it's all about inspiration and experience, right?

GREAT NICHE

Starting from the first two chapters, it's been made known to you that it's also crucial to identify the niche for your blog. What will your blog be about? What will you talk about? Would it revolve around sports, technology, or your online business? Take your pick.

Obviously, your blog's niche would be about your passion or interests. If not that, it's something that you'd like to promote. For example, comedypreneur.com is a personal blogsite of a stand-up comedian, producer, and writer named James Creviston. Because comedy is his passion, he created this blog post because he wanted to promote the world of stand-up comedy to other people, as well as make it his mission to help out aspiring stand-up comedians. Because of that in mind, he keeps creating blog posts of how-to's, tips and tricks, and advice for those who are interested in the topic.

Your passion becomes your blog's niche. Ideally, if you have a business to promote, it should technically be your passion, too. Otherwise, how else would you start a business if you weren't the least bit interested in that field?

Don't copy other people. Trust in your own knowledge and passion. Only you can add unique twists to your content. Only you can make your blog *you*. Don't feel like you have to copy Perez Hilton just because his blog (and "news") site is popular around the world. Even if you feel like your niche isn't really a popular topic in the blogging community, what's most important is that you gather a dedicated group of readers and visitors, which is the best assurance for increasing traffic. Who knows, maybe they'd be more thankful to you because you made this blog. For example, if your blog is all about knitting (and there are not many blogs focusing on that), you might even encourage more people to try it out. To have people take an interest in your passion is undoubtedly one of the best feelings in the world.

Check out other blogs in the same niche. Make no mistake, this isn't the same as "copying" other people's blogs. Once you've identified your niche, take some time checking out blogs of the same category, and try to figure out how these blogs present its content. What's unique about it? What do you like about it? What are the areas from improvement? When you get to know your specific blogging community, you'll be able to identify the things that could potentially make your blogs better. Furthermore, checking out other people's blogs might also lead you to make friends and acquaintances, people who'd also visit your blog and encourage you throughout your journey!

At the end of the day, just **stay true to yourself**. Allow your unique personality to flourish and be reflected in your blog site and posts. More than anything, your blog site is one way to express yourself. Enjoying being you; your visitors will surely appreciate you for it.

There you go. Here are the top three pieces of advice to help you with your blog. Always keep this in mind, and never lose sight of your goals. Gaining popularity for your website will not be an easy feat, but rest assured, when you incorporate all three traits—consistency, motivation, and great niche—into your blog, success will not be that far off.

CHAPTER 4

HOW TO MAKE MONEY FROM MY BLOG

Here we go, the most anticipated part of this book. In the first chapter, we've talked about how blogging is an extremely great option when trying to earn extra cash and promote your own business. Now, we will get into the step-by-step specifics.

DO WHAT YOU LOVE, THE MONEY WILL FOLLOW

This saying is perhaps the essential principle of making money through your blogs. Do what you're love. Work hard in building your site and in sharing your passion, eventually, people will take notice and appreciate your content.

It's easier to stay in business when you keep writing about the things that you love. For sure, your readers will know whether you're really interested in the topic. Everything will be evident in the quality, voice, and enthusiasm of your blog posts.

Another reason why it's easier to stay in business when you choose to blog about your passion, is that you will eventually find many people who share the same interests as you. They become dedicated to your blog and will look forward to your new content. In the long run, you'll even discover people who can become your friends. This has already been explained in the previous chapter, so you should get the picture by now.

THE DIFFERENT WAYS TO GET MONEY FROM A BLOG

For this part, we will explore the various ways with which you can earn money from your site. Read on and discover what will work best for you and your blog.

1. AFFILIATE MARKETING

First of all, you can earn your profit through **affiliate marketing**, which is considered to be the most profitable and popular method. This will only be briefly explained because there will be an upcoming guide which will dive deep into how to get started with affiliate marketing (stay tuned for that). To briefly explain, this is how it works:

- **An advertising company or single advertiser wants you to promote their products.** He or she agrees to give you a commission whenever they gain a customer coming from your blog site. You can also achieve this by something called "private partnership".

- **You will be given a link that tracks your affiliate code.** This is how the affiliate company or person knows when that customer specifically used your link to buy from them.

- **Your site will be filled with affiliate links or ads.** This can appear directly in your content (i.e. mentioning the affiliate), or through the banner ads which can be seen at the sides or bottom of your site. If visitors clicks on your unique link and buys the recommended product, you earn that commission. Of course, you helped promote the affiliate's products and services. You should definitely get some credit for that.

Besides that, you'll have to consider the following things:

- **The number of affiliate (or attached) sales highly depends on your site's number of visitors.** That's why it's smart to allot the first few weeks or months into promoting your blog and getting lots of visitors. You won't be able to earn much with affiliate marketing if you're not getting a lot of traffic yet.

- **You have to be credible enough for your visitors to click on your blog site.** This is why it's important to focus on writing about your passion because it's something you have lots of experiences and knowledge with.

- **Consider placing a notice on your "Terms and Conditions" page that you do use affiliate links.** At this point, you might be overly accustomed to seeing the "Terms and Conditions" page on a website. This is also known as "Terms of Service", "Terms of Use", or "Operating Agreement", and is essentially the contract regulating your business relationship with the advertising companies you're affiliated with.

For WordPress blog sites, there will be various plug-ins that will make your affiliate marketing easier and smoother for you. Some examples of these plug-ins are: Max Banner Ads and Max Blog Press. Google Adsense is also an extremely popular way to get into affiliate marketing. One good thing about this is that you'll get to choose the ads, and match it up with what your blog is about. Besides, it would be weird if you were talking about fashion, and the ads are all about interior design or furniture, right?

There's a lot of other technical terms and details about affiliate marketing, but let's reserve all of that for the longer, more elaborated guide.

2. GETTING PAID TO WRITE REVIEWS

This a different method from affiliate marketing. For this, you get to personally try out your affiliate's products or services—for free! Of course, the product and service should be connected to your niche, else your visitors will be experiencing some sense of confusion as to what your blog site is really all about.

Companies or businesses may approach you, or the other way around. Still, it would mean a great compliment for anyone to have affiliates directly approaches them. This means that you've already built a good reputation within your niche. If you don't know where to begin, there are also websites like PayPerHost which helps people connect them with interested businesses and companies.

For example, if your blog is all about health and wellness, you might get to write a review about a certain company's workout clothing line. They'll give you the clothes for free, and you try it out the next time you exercise. After that, you produce a blog post containing your reviews for that product. Bonus points if you honestly liked the product or service.

3. CREATING A PAID MEMBERSHIP WEBSITE

Not everyone is interested in bombarding their blog sites with various advertisements and sponsored posts. One other popular way is to create a paid membership plan for your blog site. This means that there would be areas and features in your site which will be exclusively accessed by members. It's similar to how becoming a member of a golf and country club gives you certain perks, as well as access to exclusive areas in the place.

For example, if your blog is all about creative writing, you might want to devise a paid membership plan for those who want to have access to your online creative writing courses. If your blog site is in WordPress, you can easily use a WordPress membership plug-in like MemberPress.

4. SELLING YOUR OWN EBOOKS

One way of looking at your blog sites is that it serves as revenue for you to promote unlimited content to people who are dedicated and willing to pay for it. Your blog posts may not contain everything you need to say, so one good way for you to earn extra cash is to write an e-book with more details about a certain topic related to your niche. Let's stick with the example of a blog site for creative writing. Perhaps, you can write an e-book that thoroughly delves into fiction writing or poems. Perhaps how to even become a published writer. There are numerous possibilities for this! E-books don't have to be that long, and the extra cash will be worth it.

5. SELLING YOUR OWN PRODUCTS

This works especially well if you created a blog for the sole purpose of business promotion. For example, if you're an online business that sells clothes and accessories for women, you can create a designated page in your fashion blog site just for that. It works better if you're able to maximize the promotion of your blog to your other social media accounts. If you're an artist, you can sell your paintings there.

Besides selling physical products, you can also sell digital products, such as an app on the phone or some plug-ins for video editing applications. Once again, get creative, and maximize your own potential with this.

6. HOSTING A PAID WEBINAR

Short for "web seminar", webinars is one of the sure-fire ways for you to build a bigger audience, as well as get connected with them. Since webinars are usually live or happening in real-time, you can conduct online courses while people are watching. Plus, they can ask you some questions after the session. This is an excellent way for you to gain connections and establish a relationship with your blog's dedicated fans. Who knows, your fans might even become people who will become a part of your life. More than that, this is a great way for you to get inspiration and motivation for your site.

7. OFFERING FREELANCE SERVICES

Definitely, once you and your blog has gained a reputation, people will start seeing you as credible and knowledgeable. With that, you can offer freelancer services; by connecting your service links from third-party websites like Upwork, Fiverr, or Freelancer.com.

For example, if your blog is all about video editing, perhaps you can start offering video editing services to people who need it, whether for a professional short film, a YouTube video—whatever fits your niche and expertise.

Most of these methods require a certain level of promotion on your end. Therefore, don't forget to mention your blog to your family and friends. Always have the link attached to your social media accounts, and promote your blog posts every time you publish a new one. It's a great way to stay relevant and within other people's radar.

In the blogging community, it's most important to be active in your niche. Visit other blogs and read their posts. Comment after reading their posts and encourage them that way. Chances are, they'll visit your blog too and appreciate your content.

FINAL WORDS: CONCLUSION

Definitely, trying to earn money from a blog will not happen with just one night. It requires time, effort, and dedication for you to gain some visitors. Still, because you're writing about things that you love and are passionate about, it's one of the best kinds of jobs there is.

As a start, it may be best for you to create a blog site in WordPress, and avail the shared hosting plan with a web host (preferably BlueHost). Make sure that the money you pay for the web hosting service provider will not go to waste. Work hard towards expanding your blog site's horizons, and focus on consistency, motivation, and your niche.

Stay connected with other people. Connections will be one of your greatest allies when it comes to promoting your blog. Be proud of your content and share it to the world. When it comes to fellow bloggers, keep in mind that the blogging community has this unspoken courtesy of "give and receive". How can you expect other bloggers to appreciate your content when you also don't go out of your way to read and appreciate theirs? Be proactive and don't be afraid to step out of your comfort zone. When somebody comments on your post and expresses their positive feedback about your new blog post, reply to him or her with your word of thanks. This is the best way to get dedicated visitors, and it will certainly help you in the future when you start publishing sponsored posts, selling your own products and services, and even incorporating some affiliate marketing.

You have so much potential in you. Everyone does! Turn that potential into a fulfilling profession and a good amount of income. There are endless possibilities residing in the world of blogging. Explore that and have fun with the process. Turn your passion into a profession!

We are lucky enough to live during this modern day of technology. It's easier to connect with people and share your passion with the world. It's easier to buy online products because debit or credit cards allow you to that. Even though blogging is relatively young compared to other established professions, it may as well be one of the most convenient, comfortable, and satisfying jobs. All you'll need is a little creativity and some determination—then voilà! You're now a successful blogger.

www.ingramcontent.com/pod-product-compliance
Lightning Source LLC
Chambersburg PA
CBHW050308220526
45465CB00002B/871